This book belongs to _____

Dick Bruna

Poppy Pig

Big Tent Entertainment

New York

This pig's name is Poppy Pig.

Her face is smooth and bright.

She has a funny little nose.

Her smile makes you feel all right.

The little house she lives in

has flowers on the sill.

For Poppy says, "A pot of flowers

makes a home feel nicer still."

Quite early in the morning

she ties her apron on.

Look there — now Poppy's ready,

and it is barely dawn!

Poppy Pig first sweeps the floor,

a thing she loves to do.

For Poppy says, "My house must look

all shiny clean and new."

She dusted down the cupboard next,

and took the greatest care.

She dusted up, she dusted down,

she dusted everywhere.

She dusted around the painting, too,

and hung it nice and straight.

It was so bright that Poppy thought,

"That plant looks really great."

When Poppy saw her dirty cloth,

she knew just what to do.

She rinsed it in a bowl and

used plenty of soap, too.

When the cloth was finally clean,

she hung it on the line.

Soon it was quite fresh again

and Poppy said, "That's fine."

"Oh, my!" said Poppy with a smile.

"I'm glad my cleaning is done.

I'm a little hungry now.

What can I eat for lunch that's fun?"

Poppy sliced some carrots

and put them on a plate.

"These will make me fit and strong,"

said Poppy as she ate.

Next Poppy washed the dishes,

and put them all away.

"Hurray," she said, "I'm finally done.

I've had a busy day!"

Then in her armchair Poppy sat,

and rested there with ease.

She said, "How clean my house is now.

I am really very pleased!"

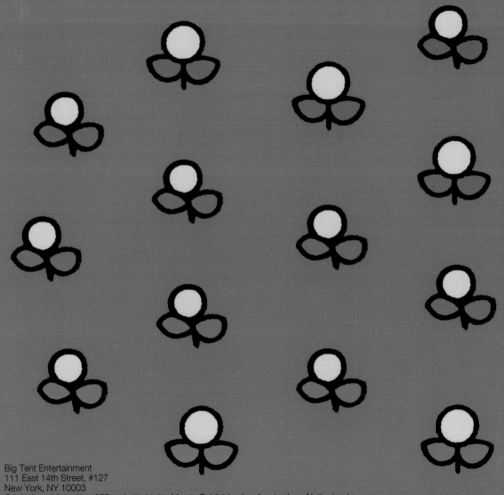

Big Tent Entertainment
111 East 14th Street, #127
New York, NY 10003
Originally published in 1977 as *betje big* by Mercis Publishing bv, Amsterdam, Netherlands.
Original text Dick Bruna © copyright by Mercis Publishing bv, 1977.
Illustrations Dick Bruna © copyright Mercis bv, 1977.
Published in the U.S. in 2003 by Big Tent Entertainment, New York.